Children will be WOWed when they dive into this fun, fact-packed series that explores the most fascinating things in the world around them. From the human body, to sharks, to insects, to atlases, to dinosaurs, there is something new and exciting to learn at every turn!

These books are anchored by the philosophy that the best form of learning is through high-quality, multi-faceted experiences. This series provides lasting knowledge as it engages children on many levels. The graphics and illustrations inspire learning in readers of all ages as they explore everything from the depths of the ocean to the cells of the human body. Students will also be captivated by the fun facts and interesting explanations, which bolster a comprehensive understanding of each subject area.

Teachers and parents alike will appreciate the significance of this series as an addition to their libraries as it promotes self-sufficiency in the learning process. With vividly portrayed information on all of children's favorite subjects, these books promote an enjoyment for both discovering and sharing knowledge, key components of a successful learning environment.

Learning should be fun, interesting, and applicable, and we are sure the young learners in your life will find this series to be all of that – and more!

"You can teach a student a lesson for a day; but if you can teach him to learn by creating curiosity, he will continue the learning process as long as he lives."

– Clay P. Bedford

© 2015 FLOWERPOT PRESS

CONTENTS UNDER LICENSE FROM
ALADDIN BOOKS LTD.

FLOWERPOT PRESS
142 2ND AVENUE NORTH
FRANKLIN, TN 37064

FLOWERPOT PRESS, A DIVISION OF KAMALU LLC, FRANKLIN,
TN, U.S.A. AND FLOWERPOT CHILDREN'S PRESS, INC.,
OAKVILLE, ON, CANADA.

ISBN 978-1-4867-0467-5

Editor
Jim Pipe

Consultant
Liz Farr

Designer
Flick Killerby

Illustrator
Stephen Sweet – Simon Girling & Associates

Picture Research
Brooks Krikler Research

American Edition Editor: Johannah Gilman Paiva
American Redesign: Jonas Fearon Bell

Printed in China.

CONTENTS

WORLD OF WONDER
WOW

I KNOW ABOUT!

THE YOUNG PEOPLE'S
ATLAS
OF THE WORLD

NAURU
YAREN

KIRIBATI
TARAWA

Equator

TUVALU
FUNAFUTI

WALLIS &
FORTUNA
ISLANDS
(France)

WESTERN
SAMOA
APIA

FIJI
SUVA

AMERICAN
SAMOA

TONGA
NUKU'ALOFA

NIUE

COOK

ISLANDS
(New Zealand)

Tropic of Capricorn

Miles 0
Kms

200

0   200   400   600

200   400   600   800

N
W   E
S

RIVERS, LAKES, *and* SWAMPS

YOUTH

Waterfalls

MATURITY

Meandering river

Delta

OLD AGE

River delta

FRESHWATER

Freshwater makes up only 3% of the world's water. However, nearly all of this water is frozen in glaciers and the ice caps found at the Poles. Only 0.01% of the world's water flows through rivers, lakes, and swamps (below).

FRESHWATER LIFE

Many rivers, swamps, and lakes teem with life from fish (above) to frogs (below). The largest freshwater fish is the pla beuk found in the Mekong River in Southeast Asia.

RIVERS

Rivers form a part of the water cycle. They act as channels, carrying rain or spring water to lakes or an ocean. As they flow, they gouge their way through rock, creating physical features such as gorges. The rock that has been eroded is carried by the river and later deposited to form features such as deltas. Near its source, a river is described as "young" (left). As it nears its destination, whether this is a lake or an ocean, it reaches "maturity," and flows from side to side in meanders. At its destination, it reaches "old age," when most of its load is deposited.

SEAS *and* OCEANS

WATERY WORLD

The seas and oceans around the world hold 97% of the world's water, and cover over two thirds of the planet's surface. The largest ocean, the Pacific, covers 63,855,000 square miles (165,383,000 sq km). The deepest point in the oceans is the Mariana Trench in the Pacific. It is nearly 7 miles (11 km) deep.

Continental shelf

Continental slope

Ocean floor

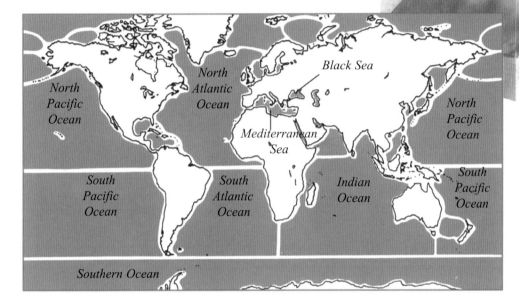

North Pacific Ocean

North Atlantic Ocean

Black Sea

Mediterranean Sea

North Pacific Ocean

South Pacific Ocean

South Atlantic Ocean

Indian Ocean

South Pacific Ocean

Southern Ocean

OCEAN FLOOR

Surrounding a landmass is a shallow part of the sea called the "continental shelf." At about 63 miles (100 km) from the shore the sea floor drops off sharply down the continental slope, before arriving at the ocean floor about 4 miles (6 km) below the surface.

LIFE BENEATH THE WAVES

The seas hold an amazing range of life. Coral reefs (below), found off the coasts of Australia, Central America, and Africa are home to animals ranging from the tiny coral to clams, stingrays, and an array of brightly colored fish. Life in the deep oceans includes microscopic plankton. These tiny organisms form the basic food supply for others from crabs (above) to enormous whales.

COASTAL EROSION

The powerful forces of the seas and oceans can have devastating effects on the rocks and soil of the coastline, eroding huge amounts from some areas and depositing them in others. The results can be stunning, with such formations as the enormous rock stacks of the Twelve Apostles on Australia's South Coast (above).

MOUNTAINS

JAGGED PEAKS

Mountains and hills are formed as the result of two crust plates colliding, causing the rock in between to be crumpled up into jagged peaks, such as the Himalayas. They may also be the result of volcanic activity, and, today, many chains of mountains still have active volcanoes, such as Mount St. Helens in Washington state (below).

Sharp mountain peaks (left), are signs of a young mountain range that has not been eroded to a great extent.

Smoother mountains (right) indicate an old mountain range. This is because they have been eroded to their present shape.

WILDLIFE

Mountain wildlife has to cope with harsh environments. Few large and ornate plants can survive the unpleasant conditions. Instead, the plants tend to be small, such as the mountain avens (above left). Mountain animals must adapt to survive. The big horn sheep of the Rocky Mountains have a thick fleece and are sure-footed climbers (right).

Plant altitudes
As the climate changes with altitude on a mountain slope, so different types of plants will grow at different heights (above and below). At the top of the highest peaks are snow and ice where little grows (1). Below this is a strip of Alpine meadow (2), containing some flowering plants and grasses. The highest trees are found in the band of coniferous evergreen forest (3). These are followed by deciduous trees (ones that shed their leaves, 4) and, if the climate is warm and wet enough, tropical cloud forest (5). Finally, there are more bands of deciduous (6) and coniferous (7) trees before giving way to open grassland at the foot of the mountain (8).

FORESTS

WOODS AND FORESTS

Large areas of land on almost every continent, with the exception of Antarctica, are covered in forests of one kind or another. These can be the enormous boreal forests (see below) that stretch across the northern regions of North America, Asia, and Europe, or the concentrations of rainforest that fill the centers of South America and Africa. These great areas of land are under threat from massive deforestation programs that clear forests at an alarming rate—up to 54,687 square miles (140,000 sq km) each year.

BOREAL FORESTS

These are found in areas with extremely cold winters and a short growing season. Also called "taiga," they generally consist of one type of tree—coniferous evergreens, such as pines (above). Despite the often harsh conditions, some animals, including the pine marten (right), thrive in boreal forests.

The world's woodlands
The large region of woodland stretching across Russia and Siberia is the largest forest on the planet. It ranges for over 6,250 miles (10,000 km) from the Baltic Sea in the east to the Pacific Ocean in the west.

Key
Temperate
Boreal
Rainforest

TEMPERATE FORESTS

These can consist of either deciduous (trees that lose their leaves) or evergreen trees. They grow in areas with warm summers, cool winters, and plenty of rainfall. They are found in areas such as Central Europe and the South. They are able to support an immense amount of wildlife, including squirrels (right) and deer.

RAINFORESTS

One of the most diverse and richly populated forms of environment, these forests are found in the warmer and wetter parts of the world, such as South America, Central Africa, and Southeast Asia. The rich growing conditions ensure the growth of a huge variety of plants that can support a large range of animal life. These animals range from tigers to brightly colored birds, such as the toucan (right).

DESERTS

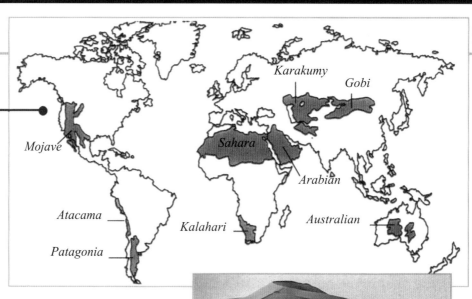

DESERTS

Although generally thought of as hot areas, the word "desert" applies to any region with very little rainfall. Deserts cover about 14 percent of the Earth's land area, the largest being the Sahara in North Africa. Of these deserts, only 10 to 20 percent are actually covered in sand.

Sand dunes
Dunes (right) are formed by wind blowing over sand in the same way as wind causes waves when it blows over water. Sand dunes can be up to 1,525 feet (465 m) high and 3 miles (5 km) long.

Animals of the desert
Creatures that have to live in the desert have developed special physical features and actions that suit the harsh climate. Camels (top) have large, padded feet to stop them from sinking into the sand and long eyelashes to stop sand from being blown into their eyes. The Fennec fox (right) has large ears to help it keep cool. Desert lizards (above) need the warm weather to survive. However, too much heat can be fatal. To escape the harsh sun, the lizard burrows into the cool ground.

Water vapor condenses and forms clouds

Warm moist air rises and cools

Rain falls and the rain clouds disappear, forming rain-shadow zone.

Dry air warms up as it sinks

RAIN SHADOW

Some deserts, such as the Atacama in South America, are called rain-shadow deserts. They are usually found behind a chain of mountains. As warm, moist air blows into the mountain chain, it rises and cools. As it cools, the air is unable to hold onto its water, which forms clouds and then falls as rain. As the now dry air passes over the mountains, it falls and gets warmer, creating a warm, dry area, or rain-shadow zone (above).

ICE SHEETS *and* TUNDRA

THE POLES

The extremes at either end of the Earth are very cold places that have to endure extended periods of darkness during the winter. The landscape here is dominated by large, moving ice sheets. Farther away from the Poles, the ice sheets, give way to tundra, a treeless landscape, where only grasses and mosses can grow above a permanently frozen subsoil.

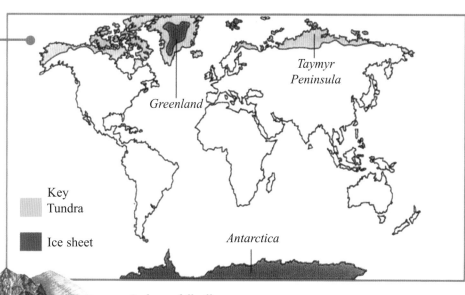

Taymyr Peninsula

Greenland

Key
Tundra

Ice sheet

Antarctica

Glacier

Icebergs fall off

Iceberg

Glaciers
Glaciers spread out from a source. As the glacier approaches the warmer waters of the sea, cracks form. These cracks grow and eventually large chunks of ice fall off to form icebergs (left).

Cracks multiply as ice nears sea

ICE SHEETS

The area around the North Pole, the Arctic, has no land. Instead, the Arctic Ocean is covered by an immense ice sheet which varies in size with the changing seasons. The South Pole, or Antarctica, is the coldest continent on the planet. Like the Arctic, the area is covered by thick sheets of ice all year round. However, beneath the ice is a large landmass complete with mountain ranges (see page 29).

Animals of the cold
Many animals, such as the Arctic fox (above), change the color of their coats with the seasons. In summer they are dark, while in winter they are white to match the snow. The musk ox (right) has a large, shaggy coat to keep it warm.

TUNDRA

Because the tundra regions have long, cold winters and short summers, trees cannot grow in these regions (left). About 12 inches (30 cm) below the surface, the soil is frozen all year round. This frozen soil is known as "permafrost" and it stops water draining from the surface, keeping the soil boggy. Other tundra features include pingoes.

Ice

Gas Pressure

Pingoes
Pingoes are bulges in the ground caused by the earth being forced up by a buildup of gas beneath the ice.

11

GRASSLANDS

The steppes of Asia cover an enormous area, stretching from the Ukraine to Siberia. The world's largest prairie region is in North America, while almost two-fifths of Africa is covered by savanna (left).

Russian Steppes

North American Prairie

Sahel

African Savanna

Pampas

GRASSLANDS

Grasslands occupy large areas of land within the larger continents. Examples include the steppes of Central Asia, the prairies of North America, the Pampas of South America, and the savanna of southern Africa.

There are three types of grassland (steppe, prairie, and savanna—see below) and they often lie between desert and rich forested areas. Much of these grasslands has been turned over to farming, usually grazing livestock.

WILDLIFE

Despite the lack of significant tree cover, grasslands hold a rich and diverse range of animal life. These include herds of grazing animals that migrate across them in search of food, such as the giraffe (above) and zebra (below) of Africa and the pronghorn of North America. Animals that do not migrate also live in grasslands. Prairie dogs (bottom left) live in burrows on the North American Prairie.

TYPES OF GRASSLAND

Savanna is scattered with trees and shrubs, including acacias and baobabs. Its grass does not totally cover the ground, growing, instead, in clumps. These regions may also endure long drought periods. Prairies have often been referred to as "seas of grass." They are covered in long grasses with flowers, while trees such as cottonwood and willows are restricted to river valleys. The steppes are covered in very short grasses and found in dry areas with hot summers and cold winters.

The MAPS

The following section looks at the world in more detail. Each chapter examines a different region, from North America to Australia and the Poles. Comprehensive maps reveal each region's physical features, and highlight a few cultural, economic, and political points of interest. Each map also shows the flags of the nations, their capitals, and other major cities.

Accompanying text describes the region's countryside and points out individual physical features, such as the length of major rivers and the altitude of the highest mountains to present a full view of the world's continents.

Area shown by map

Country flag and name

Country name

Seas and Oceans

Text about continent

Capital city

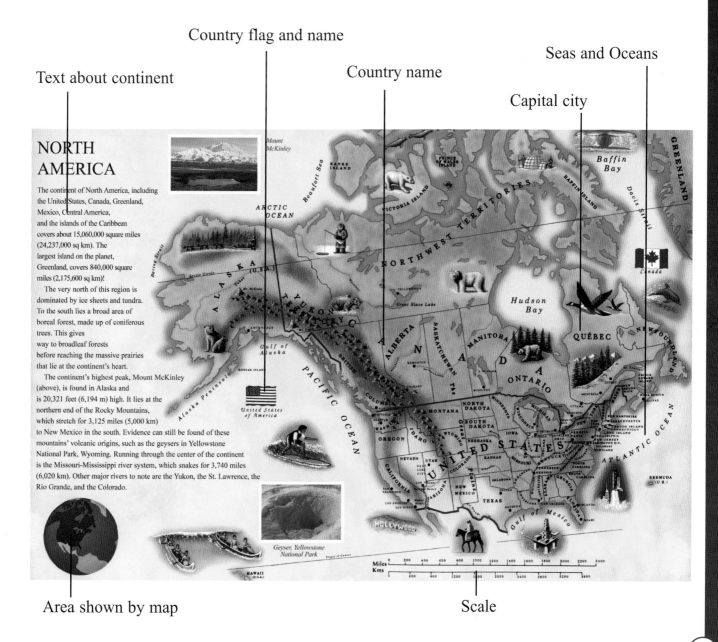

NORTH AMERICA

The continent of North America, including the United States, Canada, Greenland, Mexico, Central America, and the islands of the Caribbean covers about 15,060,000 square miles (24,237,000 sq km). The largest island on the planet, Greenland, covers 840,000 square miles (2,175,600 sq km)!

The very north of this region is dominated by ice sheets and tundra. To the south lies a broad area of boreal forest, made up of coniferous trees. This gives way to broadleaf forests before reaching the massive prairies that lie at the continent's heart.

The continent's highest peak, Mount McKinley (above), is found in Alaska and is 20,321 feet (6,194 m) high. It lies at the northern end of the Rocky Mountains, which stretch for 3,125 miles (5,000 km) to New Mexico in the south. Evidence can still be found of these mountains' volcanic origins, such as the geysers in Yellowstone National Park, Wyoming. Running through the center of the continent is the Missouri-Mississippi river system, which snakes for 3,740 miles (6,020 km). Other major rivers to note are the Yukon, the St. Lawrence, the Rio Grande, and the Colorado.

Geyser, Yellowstone National Park

Area shown by map

Scale

NORTH AMERICA

Mount McKinley

The continent of North America, including the United States, Canada, Greenland, Mexico, Central America, and the islands of the Caribbean covers about 15,060,000 square miles (24,237,000 sq km). The largest island on the planet, Greenland, covers 840,000 square miles (2,175,600 sq km)!

The very north of this region is dominated by ice sheets and tundra. To the south lies a broad area of boreal forest, made up of coniferous trees. This gives way to broadleaf forests before reaching the massive prairies that lie at the continent's heart.

The continent's highest peak, Mount McKinley (above), is found in Alaska and is 20,321 feet (6,194 m) high. It lies at the northern end of the Rocky Mountains, which stretch for 3,125 miles (5,000 km) to New Mexico in the south. Evidence can still be found of these mountains' volcanic origins, such as the geysers in Yellowstone National Park, Wyoming. Running through the center of the continent is the Missouri-Mississippi river system, which snakes for 3,740 miles (6,020 km). Other major rivers to note are the Yukon, the St. Lawrence, the Rio Grande, and the Colorado.

Geyser, Yellowstone National Park

PRINCE OF WALES ISLAND

Baffin Bay

GREENLAND

NORTHWEST TERRITORIES

VICTORIA ISLAND

BAFFIN ISLAND

Davis Strait

Canada

YELLOWKNIFE

Great Slave Lake

Hudson Bay

ALBERTA

SASKATCHEWAN

The

MANITOBA

QUÉBEC

NEWFOUNDLAND

C A N A D A

EDMONTON

Athabasca

Saskatchewan

L. Winnipeg

ONTARIO

St. Lawrence

PRINCE EDWARD ISLAND

CALGARY

WINNIPEG

Québec

NEW BRUNSWICK

NOVA SCOTIA

HALIFAX

COLUMBIA

VANCOUVER

MONTANA

NORTH DAKOTA

Missouri

L. Superior

MICHIGAN

L. Huron

OTTAWA

MONTRÉAL

VICTORIA

WASHINGTON

SEATTLE

SOUTH DAKOTA

MINNESOTA

WISCONSIN

L. Michigan

Niagara Falls

MAINE

NEW HAMPSHIRE

VERMONT

NEW YORK

MASSACHUSETTS

RHODE ISLAND

CONNECTICUT

LONG ISLAND

OREGON

IDAHO

WYOMING

Great

NEBRASKA

IOWA

Missouri

CHICAGO

DETROIT

CLEVELAND

OHIO

PITTSBURGH

PENNSYL-VANIA

NEW YORK CITY

PHILADELPHIA

NEW JERSEY

WASHINGTON D.C.

DELAWARE

MARYLAND

NEVADA

UTAH

SALT LAKE CITY

COLORADO

KANSAS

Arkansas

MISSOURI

ST. LOUIS

Ohio

INDIANA

KENTUCKY

WEST VIRGINIA

VIRGINIA

U N I T E D   S T A T E S

CALIFORNIA

SAN FRANCISCO

LAS VEGAS

Painted Desert

ARIZONA

Colorado

NEW MEXICO

Plains

OKLAHOMA

Arkansas

TENNESSEE

MEMPHIS

Mississippi

ALABAMA

Appalachians

NORTH CAROLINA

SOUTH CAROLINA

GEORGIA

ATLANTIC OCEAN

BERMUDA (U.K.)

LOS ANGELES

SAN DIEGO

Mojave Desert

Rio Grande

TEXAS

DALLAS

HOUSTON

LOUISIANA

Mississippi

NEW ORLEANS

FLORIDA

ORLANDO

MIAMI

HOLLYWOOD

Gulf of Mexico

Miles

0 200 400 600 800 1000 1200 1400 1600 1800 2000 2200 2400

Kms

0 400 800 1200 1600 2000 2400 2800 3200 3600

15

NASSAU
BAHAMAS

Tropic of Cancer

PUERTO RICO
SAN JUAN

Straits of Florida

SANTO DOMINGO
HAITI
PORT AU PRINCE
DOMINICAN REPUBLIC

HAVANA • CUBA

Gulf of Mexico

Yucatan Channel

CAYMAN ISLANDS
KINGSTON

JAMAICA

ARUBA

Caribbean Sea

Sierra Madre Oriental

MEXICO

Sierra Madre Occidental

Mt. Popocatepetl

BELIZE
BELMOPAN

HONDURAS
TEGUCIGALPA

NICARAGUA
MANAGUA

PANAMA CITY
Panama Canal

GUATEMALA CITY

MEXICO CITY • Mt. Orizaba

GUATEMALA
SAN SALVADOR
EL SALVADOR

SAN JOSÉ
L. Nicaragua
COSTA RICA

PANAMA

BOGOTÁ

COLOMBIA

QUITO

ECUADOR

Ecuador

GALAPAGOS ISLANDS
(Ecuador)

SOUTH *and* CENTRAL AMERICA

Linking the two continents of North and South America is the narrow strip of land called Central America. This region's countryside changes from scrub and desert in the north of Mexico to lush, tropical rainforest which stretches from the Yucatan Peninsula all the way to South America.

To the east is the Caribbean Sea, which is home to hundreds of islands. These lie in an arc from Cuba and the Bahamas in the north, to Trinidad and Tobago just off the coast of Venezuela.

South America itself contains one of the world's largest river systems. The Amazon winds for 4,073 miles (6,450 km) from the Andes to the Atlantic. Its river basin covers 4.5 million square miles (7 million sq km), has more than 200 tributaries, and is mostly covered in dense rainforest (see page 9). South America also has the world's longest mountain chain, the Andes, stretching for 4,500 miles (7,250 km) from Panama to Cape Horn. They include the continent's tallest peak, Aconcagua, whose summit is 22,834 feet (6,960 m) high.

Peru

Bolivia

Chile

The Andes

Argentina

Paraguay

Miles	0	200	400	600	800
Kms	0	400	800	1200	

ATLANTIC OCEAN

ANGUILLA
ANTIGUA AND BARBUDA
GUADELOUPE
DOMINICA
ST.KITTS
& NEVIS   MARTINIQUE
ST.LUCIA   BARBADOS
ST.VINCENT & THE GRENADINES
GRENADA

PORT OF SPAIN
TRINIDAD & TOBAGO
PARAMARIBO   CAYENNE
GEORGETOWN
CARACAS
VENEZUELA   GUYANA   SURINAM   FRENCH GUIANA
Orinoco

Equator

Colombia

French Guiana

Cuba

Bahamas

Dominican Republic

Jamaica

Brazil

BRAZIL

BRASILIA

S. Francisco

Amazon

PERU

BOLIVIA

Mato Grosso

Paraná

RIO DE JANEIRO

Tropic of Capricorn

Honduras

Costa Rica

Belize

Panama

Antigua & Barbuda

L. Titicaca

LIMA   LA PAZ

PARAGUAY

ASUNCION

Paraguay

ARGENTINA

Atacama Desert

Mt Ojos del Salado

Uruguay

URUGUAY

MONTEVIDEO

BUENOS AIRES

Pampas

St.Kitts & Nevis

Dominica

Martinique

Barbados

St.Vincent & the Grenadines

Trinidad & Tobago

PACIFIC OCEAN

CHILE

Mt Aconcagua

SANTIAGO

Uruguay

Venezuela

Guyana

St.Lucia

Surinam

Patagonia

ATLANTIC OCEAN

El Salvador

Nicaragua

Haiti

Guatemala

Grenada

FALKLAND ISLANDS
(U.K.)

Strait of Magellan

Tierra del Fuego

17

Sweden

Norway

United Kingdom

Estonia

Latvia

Finland

ICELAND
REYKJAVIK

RUSSIAN

Lake Onega

Lake Ladoga

HELSINKI

ST. PETERSBURG

FAROE ISLANDS

Denmark

SHETLAND ISLANDS

ORKNEY ISLANDS

OSLO

STOCKHOLM

TALLINN

ESTONIA

MOSCOW

North Sea

Lake Vänern

Lake Vättern

Baltic Sea

RIGA

LATVIA

Russia

HEBRIDES

SCOTLAND

EDINBURGH

Pennines

LITHUANIA

VILNIUS

BELARUS

MINSK

NORTHERN IRELAND

BELFAST

DENMARK

COPENHAGEN

DUBLIN

UNITED KINGDOM

ENGLAND

AMSTERDAM

NETHERLANDS

BERLIN

POLAND

WARSAW

KIEV

Dneper

REPUBLIC OF IRELAND

Shannon

WALES

Severn

GERMANY

Elbe

UKRAINE

Irish Sea

CARDIFF

LONDON

Thames

BRUSSELS

BELGIUM

Rhine

PRAGUE

CZECH REPUBLIC

SLOVAKIA

Dniester

MOLDOVA

LUXEMBOURG

BRATISLAVA

KISHINEV

English Channel

Seine

VIENNA

LIECHTENSTEIN

VADUZ

AUSTRIA

Lake Balaton

BUDAPEST

HUNGARY

ROMANIA

Sea of Azov

PARIS

FRANCE

Loire

BERNE

SWITZERLAND

SLOVENIA

LJUBLJANA

ZAGREB

BUCHAREST

ATLANTIC OCEAN

Bay of Biscay

Garonne

Rhône

L. Geneva

Alps

Po

ITALY

CROATIA

Apennines

SARAJEVO

BELGRADE

Danube

Black

SERBIA

BULGARIA

SAN MARINO

BOSNIA AND HERZEGOVINA

KOSOVO

SOFIA

ISTANBUL

MONACO

VATICAN CITY STATE

ROME

TIRANA

SKOPJE

MACEDONIA

ALBANIA

Adriatic Sea

Pyrénées Mts.

ANDORRA LA VELLA

CORSICA

ANDORRA

GREECE

Aegean Sea

ANKARA

TURKEY

SPAIN

MADRID

SARDINIA

NICOSIA

CYPRUS

PORTUGAL

Guadalquivir

BALEARIC ISLANDS

ATHENS

PAROS

LISBON

SICILY

VALLETTA

MALTA

CRETE

GIBRALTAR

Strait of Gibraltar

Malta

Greece

Mediterranean Sea

18

EUROPE

Europe, including the Russian Federation to the Urals, covers 4,052,000 square miles (10,498,000 sq km).

The far north of the continent lies within the Arctic Circle, which is dominated by tundra (see page 11). Farther south, the majority of the continent is taken up by the European plain, a large belt of fertile land, much of which has been turned over to farming (above). To the south, the region is covered by Mediterranean scrubland.

Major European mountain chains include the Urals, which divide the continent from Asia, the Pyrenees between France and Spain, the Alps in Central Europe, and the Carpathians to the east. Major rivers include the Rhine, the Rhône, the Danube, the Volga, and the Vistula.

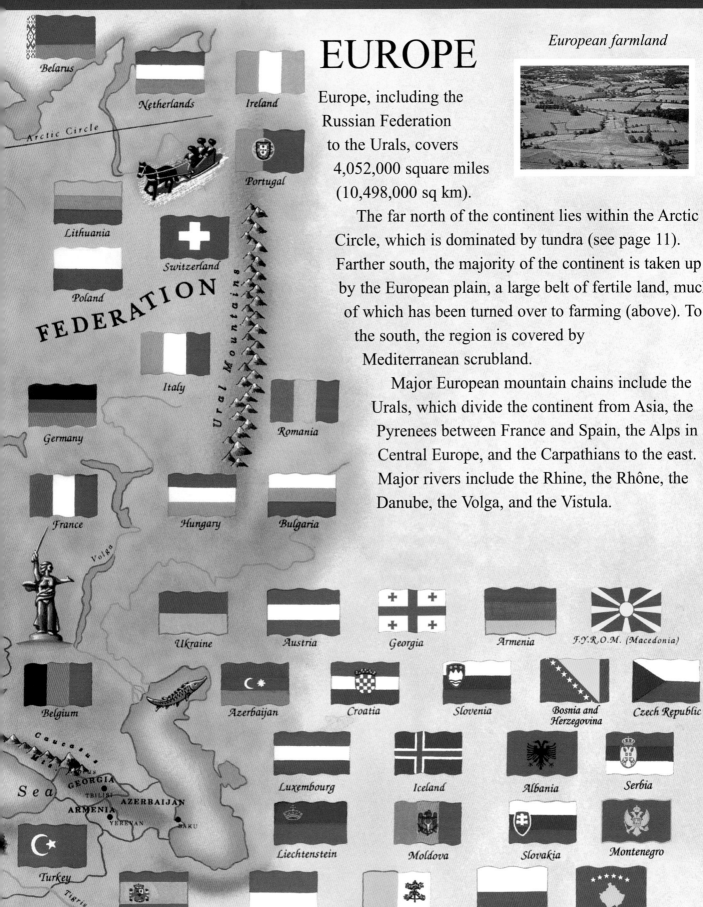

Belarus

Netherlands

Ireland

Portugal

Lithuania

Switzerland

Poland

FEDERATION

Italy

Ural Mountains

Romania

Germany

France

Hungary

Bulgaria

Volga

Ukraine

Austria

Georgia

Armenia

F.Y.R.O.M. (Macedonia)

Belgium

Azerbaijan

Croatia

Slovenia

Bosnia and Herzegovina

Czech Republic

Caucasus

Sea

GEORGIA
TBILISI
ARMENIA
AZERBAIJAN
YEREVAN
BAKU

Luxembourg

Iceland

Albania

Serbia

Turkey

Tigris

Liechtenstein

Moldova

Slovakia

Montenegro

Spain

Monaco

Vatican City State

San Marino

Kosovo

Cyprus

Andorra

Miles					
0	200	400	600	800	

Kms						
0	200	400	600	800	1000	1200	1400

Morocco

Tunisia

Mauritania

Israel

Lebanon

Syria

Egypt

Jordan

MADEIRA
FUNCHAL

CANARY ISLANDS
(Spain)

ATLANTIC OCEAN

ALGIERS
RABAT
Atlas Mountains

TUNIS
TUNISIA

Mediterranean Sea

TRIPOLI

SYRIA
BEIRUT
LEBANON
DAMASCUS
AMMAN
JERUSALEM
ISRAEL
JORDAN

Algeria

Libya

LIBYA

CAIRO

EGYPT

Red Sea

MOROCCO
EL AAION
WESTERN
SAHARA

ALGERIA

Libyan Desert

Nile

Sahara Desert

MAURITANIA
NOUAKCHOTT

MALI

NIGER

CHAD

Chad

Sudan

ERITREA

SENEGAL
DAKAR
THE
GAMBIA
BANJUL

Niger

NIAMEY

Niger

Lake
Chad

N'DJAMENA

SUDAN

KHARTOUM
Blue Nile

ETHIOPIA
ADDIS
ABABA

BISSAU
GUINEA-
BISSAU
CONAKRY
FREETOWN
SIERRA LEONE
MONROVIA
LIBERIA

GUINEA
BAMAKO
OUAGADOUGOU
BURKINA FASO

CÔTE
D'IVOIRE
YAMOUSSOUKRO

GHANA
TOGO
BENIN
ACCRA
PORTO
NOVO
LOME

NIGERIA
ABUJA
LAGOS

CAMEROON

CENTRAL
AFRICAN REPUBLIC
BANGUI

SOUTH
SUDAN

Nile

Senegal

Ghana

Burkina Faso

EQUATORIAL GUINEA
SAO TOME
MALABO
YAOUNDE
LIBREVILLE
SAO
TOME
PRINCIPE
GABON
R CONGO
BRAZZAVILLE

DR CONGO

KIGALI
RWANDA
BUJUMBURA
BURUNDI

UGANDA
KAMPALA

KENYA

NAIROBI

Lake
Victoria
ZANZIBAR

Gambia

ASCENSION

KINSHASA
DEMOCRATIC REPUBLIC OF
THE CONGO

TANZANIA
DODOMA

Guinea-Bissau

Nigeria

Côte d'Ivoire

Democratic Republic
of the Congo
DR'C

LUANDA

ANGOLA

ZAMBIA
LUSAKA

LILONGWE
MALAWI
Lake
Nyasa

MOZAMBIQUE

Guinea

Liberia

ST HELENA

ATLANTIC OCEAN

HARARE
ZIMBABWE

Sierra Leone

Mali

Togo

Tropic of
Capricorn

NAMIBIA

WINDHOEK

BOTSWANA

GABORONE

PRETORIA

MAPUTO
MBABANE

Benin

Gabon

SWAZILAND

SOUTH AFRICA

MASERU
LESOTHO

Cameroon

Equatorial Guinea

Cape of
Good
Hope

South Africa

AFRICA *and the* MIDDLE EAST

African savanna

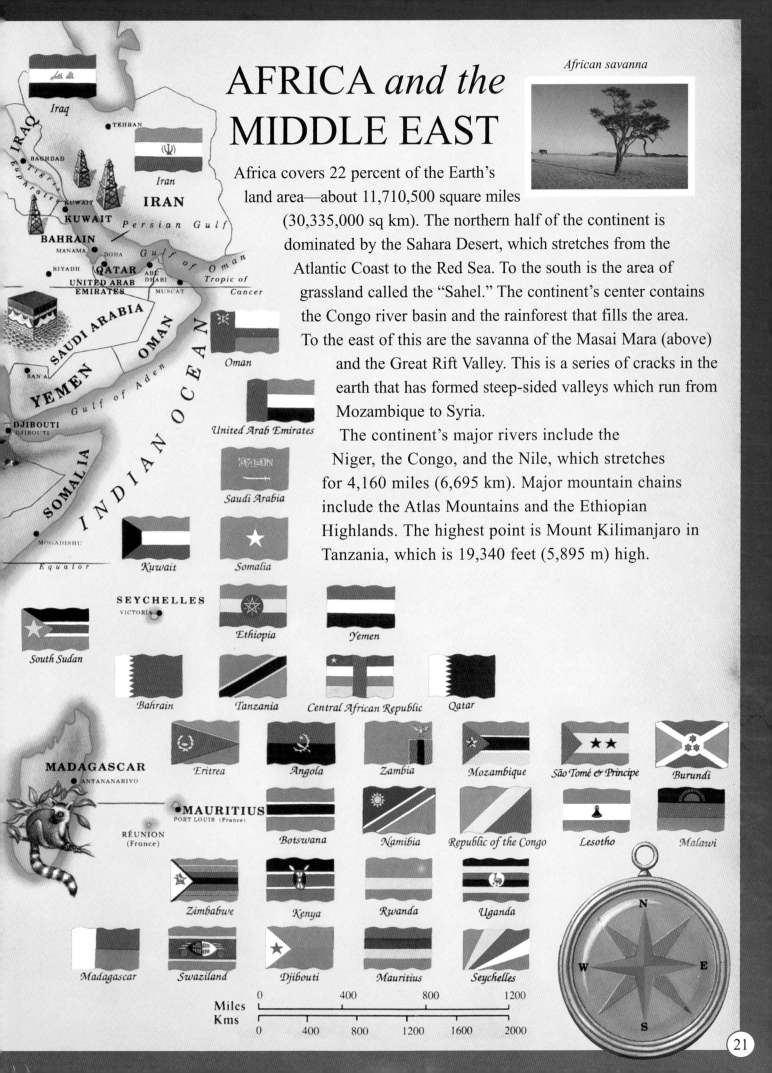

Africa covers 22 percent of the Earth's land area—about 11,710,500 square miles (30,335,000 sq km). The northern half of the continent is dominated by the Sahara Desert, which stretches from the Atlantic Coast to the Red Sea. To the south is the area of grassland called the "Sahel." The continent's center contains the Congo river basin and the rainforest that fills the area. To the east of this are the savanna of the Masai Mara (above) and the Great Rift Valley. This is a series of cracks in the earth that has formed steep-sided valleys which run from Mozambique to Syria.

The continent's major rivers include the Niger, the Congo, and the Nile, which stretches for 4,160 miles (6,695 km). Major mountain chains include the Atlas Mountains and the Ethiopian Highlands. The highest point is Mount Kilimanjaro in Tanzania, which is 19,340 feet (5,895 m) high.

Iraq
TEHRAN
Iran
IRAN
BAGHDAD
KUWAIT
KUWAIT
Persian Gulf
BAHRAIN
MANAMA
DOHA
Gulf of Oman
RIYADH
QATAR
ABU DHABI
Muscat
Tropic of Cancer
UNITED ARAB EMIRATES
SAUDI ARABIA
OMAN
Oman
YEMEN
San'a
United Arab Emirates
Gulf of Aden
DJIBOUTI
DJIBOUTI
Saudi Arabia
SOMALIA
INDIAN OCEAN
MOGADISHU
Kuwait
Somalia
Equator
SEYCHELLES
VICTORIA
Ethiopia
Yemen
South Sudan
Bahrain
Tanzania
Central African Republic
Qatar
MADAGASCAR
ANTANANARIVO
Eritrea
Angola
Zambia
Mozambique
São Tomé & Principe
Burundi
MAURITIUS
PORT LOUIS (France)
RÉUNION
(France)
Botswana
Namibia
Republic of the Congo
Lesotho
Malawi
Zimbabwe
Kenya
Rwanda
Uganda
Madagascar
Swaziland
Djibouti
Mauritius
Seychelles

Miles	0	400	800	1200
Kms	0	400 800	1200 1600	2000

N
W   E
S

21

Mount Fuji, Japan

NORTHERN ASIA

Sitting within the Arctic Circle, the north of this continent is covered in tundra (see page 11). Below this lies a large band of boreal forest, or taiga (see page 9). Sitting in the center of the continent is the Gobi Desert, which covers 50,781 square miles (1.3 million sq km). Surrounding this dry area are wide tracts of grasslands, known as steppes (see page 12).

Major rivers include the Volga and the Chang Jiang (Yangtze), which is 3,430 miles (6,380 km) long.

The eastern coast of Asia sits on the edge of the Ring of Fire.

It has seen a great deal of volcanic activity, that has over millions of years created peaks such as Mount Fuji in Japan (above).

BARENTS SEA

Kara Sea

RUSSIAN FEDERATION

Yenisey

Ob

NOVOSIBIRSK

OMSK

Irtysh

Ural Mountains

Volga

Ural

MOSCOW

KAZAKHSTAN

Lake Balkhash

Takliman (Desert)

ALMA-ATA

Aral Sea

BISHKEK

KYRGYZSTAN

Pamir

UZBEKISTAN

TASHKENT

DUSHANBE

Karakumy Desert

TAJIKISTAN

Caspian Sea

TURKMENISTAN

ASHGABAT

Mountains

Himalayas

Tajikistan

Mac

Laptev Sea

East Siberian Sea

Bering Strait

Arctic Circle

RUSSIAN FEDERATION

YAKUTSK •

Lena

Russian
Federation

Sea of
Okhotsk

Trans-Siberian Railway

Mongolia

IRKUTSK • Lake Baikal

North Korea

ULAN BATOR •

MONGOLIA
Gobi Desert

Hokkaido

VLADIVOSTOK •

Honshu

NORTH KOREA
PYONGYANG •

SEOUL •
BEIJING •   SOUTH
                  KOREA

Great Wall of China

Huang He

Yellow Sea

Sea of Japan

Shikoku

Kyushu

Mt. Fuji TOKYO •

JAPAN

PACIFIC OCEAN

Japan

South Korea

Taiwan

Turkmenistan

SHANGHAI •

Chang Jiang (Yangtze)

East China
Sea

Tropic of Cancer

CHINA

TAIPEI •
TAIWAN

MACAU • • HONG KONG

Kazakhstan

Kyrgyzstan

Hong Kong

Uzbekistan

Miles

Kms

0   200   300   400   500

0   200 300 400 500 600 700 800

China

N
E
W
S

23

Laos

Bangladesh

Vietnam

Malaysia

Burma

Nepal

Bhutan

Brunei

Karakoram Mts.

HUNZA

TIBET

AFGHANISTAN

KABUL   ISLAMABAD

LHASA

Singapore

Himalayas

Mt. Everest

NEPAL

THIMPHU

Maldives

NEW DELHI

KATHMANDU   BHUTAN

P A K I S T A N

Brahmaputra

Indus

Ganges

Yamuna

Afghanistan

KARACHI

INDIA

KOLKATA

DHAKA   BURMA

Arabian
Sea

Bay of
Bengal

YANGON

Pakistan

MUMBAI

Eastern Ghats

India

ANDAMAN
ISLANDS
(India)

Western Ghats

SRI
LANKA

I N D I A N

SINGAPORE

FIVE
HUNDRED

$500

$500

COLOMBO

5000197

MALE

O C E A N

RESERVE

50

MALDIVES

Equator

50

9RE 403163

N

W   E

S

Cambodia

Thailand

Sri Lanka

24

SOUTH *and* SOUTHEAST ASIA

Terraced rice paddies

South and Southeast Asia are lush and fertile places. Apart from the desert area in western Pakistan and the scrublands of Central India, the region is rich in fertile farmland (left) and tropical vegetation.

The major rivers include the Ganges, which flows from the Himalayas to the Indian Ocean at Bangladesh, and the Mekong, which is 2,749 miles (4,425 km) long.

The major mountain chain in this region is the range called the Himalayas. These lie just south of the Himalayan Plateau and stretch for over 1,500 miles (2,400 km). They contain the world's highest peak—Mt. Everest, which is 29,028 feet (8,848 m) high. The region of sea between the Pacific and the Indian Ocean is filled with thousands of islands—Indonesia alone is made up of over 13,600 islands, including Java and Sumatra.

Tropic of Cancer

HANOI

LUZON

L A O S

VIENTIANE

Mekong

PHILIPPINES

THAILAND

VIETNAM

South China Sea

MANILA

Chao Phraya

BANGKOK

CAMBODIA

PHNOM PENH

HO CHI MINH CITY

Gulf of Thailand

P A C I F I C   O C E A N

MINDANAO

SABAH

Philippines

BANDAR SERI BEGAWAN

Celebes Sea

MALAYSIA

BRUNEI

Strait of Malacca

KUALA LUMPUR

SARAWAK

Moluccas

SUMATRA

SINGAPORE

BORNEO

SULAWESI

IRIAN JAYA

I N D O N E S I A

Flores Sea

JAKARTA

JAVA

BALI

Indonesia

Miles	0	200		400		600		800		1000		1200
Kms	0	200	400	600	800	1000	1200	1400	1600	1800	2000

Papua New Guinea

Solomon Islands

IRIAN JAYA

PAPUA NEW GUINEA

SOLOMON ISLANDS

PORT MORESBY

Coral Sea

Gulf of Carpentaria

INDIAN OCEAN

DARWIN

Great Barrier Reef

NORTHERN TERRITORY

The Great Dividing Range

Great Sandy Desert

QUEENSLAND

Simpson Desert

ALICE SPRINGS

AUSTRALIA

Ayers Rock

Gibson Desert

Great Artesian Basin

BRISBANE

WESTERN AUSTRALIA

Great Victoria Desert

Darling

NEW SOUTH WALES

SOUTH AUSTRALIA

SYDNEY

CANBERRA

Mt. Kosciusko

PERTH

Great Australian Bight

ADELAIDE

Murray

VICTORIA

SOUTHERN OCEAN

MELBOURNE

Bass Strait

Australia

TASMANIA

HOBART

Western Samoa

Miles	0	200	400	600	800
Kms	0	200	400	600	800	1000	1200

The PACIFIC ISLANDS and AUSTRALIA

Coral atoll

The country of Australia forms the world's smallest continent, covering 2,966,200 square miles (7,682,300 sq km). The majority of the country's interior is covered in scrub and desert, notably the Great Sandy and the Great Victoria Deserts. To the north, the climate is more tropical, supporting lush rainforest. Running north to south along the eastern edge of the country is the Great Dividing Range. At the southern end of this range is the continent's highest point, Mount Kosciusko, which is 7,316 feet (2,230 m). The longest river is the Murray-Darling system, at 2,310 miles (3,717 km) long. New Zealand's climate is far cooler than Australia's—its southern coast reflects the fjord landscape of northern Europe. The Pacific Ocean holds hundreds of tiny islands, such as those of Western Samoa. Many of these islands are coral atolls—huge structures formed by the skeletons of tiny animals.

HONIARA

Vanuatu

VANUATU
PORT
VILA

NEW
CALEDONIA
(France)

NOUMÉA

Capricorn

Tropic of

PACIFIC OCEAN

EASTER ISLAND
(Chile)

Fiji

Kiribati

Nauru

NORTH
ISLAND

NEW ZEALAND

WELLINGTON

SOUTH
ISLAND

Cook Strait

Mt. Cook ● CHRISTCHURCH

Tasman Sea

New Zealand

Tonga

Tuvalu

● NAURU
YAREN

KIRIBATI
TARAWA

Equator

TUVALU
FUNAFUTI

WALLIS &
FORTUNA
ISLANDS
(France)

WESTERN
SAMOA

APIA

FIJI
● SUVA

AMERICAN
SAMOA

Tropic of Capricorn

TONGA
NUKU'ALOFA

NIUE

COOK
ISLANDS
(New Zealand)

Miles   0
Kms
         0   200
             200   400
                200   400   600
                  400 600
                      800

ANTARCTICA

Antarctic Peninsula

This continent, including the ice cap that stretches into the Southern Ocean in many places, covers about 5,468,750 square miles (14,000,000 sq km). The ice sheet averages about 6,800 feet (2,200 m) thick, and can reach 14,800 feet (4,800 m) deep. The continent is also the place where the world's lowest natural temperature was recorded—an astonishing -128.6°F (-89.2°C). Normally, the temperature rarely reaches above 32°F (0°C). Antarctica has no rivers, but does contain mountain chains such as the Transantarctic Mountains and the highest point, the Vinson Massif, at 15,900 feet (5,140 m) high.

SOUTH GEORGIA (U.K.)

NORWEGIAN DEPENDENCY

Extent of pack-ice

FALKLAND ISLANDS
Stanley (U.K.)

SOUTH ORKNEY (U.K.)

BRITISH ANTARCTIC TERRITORY

ARGENTINA

CHILE

ANTARCTIC PENINSULA

Weddell Sea

Argentinian claim

DRONNING MAUD LAND

AUSTRALIAN ANTARCTIC TERRITORY

Bellingshausen Sea

Argentinian claim

Chilean claim

Vinson Massif

SOUTH POLE

Transantarctic Mts.

PACIFIC OCEAN

MARIE BYRD LAND

Amundsen Sea

Ross Ice Shelf

McMurdo Sound

(France)

Antarctic Circle

Ross Sea

ROSS DEPENDENCY (New Zealand)

(Australia)

Miles 0 200 400 600 800
Kms 0 400 800 1200

Miles | 0 | 200 | 400 | 800
Kms | 0 | 400 | 800 | 1200

RUSSIAN FEDERATION

Barents Sea

NORWAY

Laptev Sea

ARCTIC OCEAN

SVALBARD (Norway)

+ NORTH POLE

Extent of pack-ice

ICELAND Norwegian Sea

WRANGEL ISLAND (Russia)

Bering Strait

Chukchi Sea

ALASKA (U.S.A.)

Beaufort Sea

QUEEN ELIZABETH ISLANDS

GREENLAND

CANADA

BAFFIN ISLAND

Arctic glacier

ARCTIC

The region known as the Arctic consists of the Arctic Ocean and numerous islands, including Greenland and Wrangel Island—there is no single continental landmass. The North Pole sits in the center of this frozen ocean. The Arctic Ocean, the world's smallest ocean, covers about 5,440,000 square miles (14,090,000 sq km), and most of this lies under ice throughout the year. This pack ice increases in size during the winter months, when most of the region is in darkness while the sun remains below the horizon. This is because the Earth spins around the sun at an angle, keeping the North Pole in shade during the winter months. Beyond the ice sheet, the surrounding islands are covered with a tundra landscape (see page 11), which frequently blooms with flowers during the milder summer months.

INDEX